Angel Wings Oracle Cards

Messages from the Archangels, Ascended Masters & Mother Earth

Welcome to the second set of oracle cards, these cards offer high vibrational energy healing.
You can use these for daily guidance and support, meditation, place under your pillow or use as a coaster. With the healing energies of the Archangels, Ascended Masters & Mother Earth

Nature Intuitive
EnergyHealer

Fairy Energy

The Fairies remind you to heal your inner child with compassion and playfulness

Archangel Sandalphon

Archangel Sandalphon offers you
comfort with his beautiful wings
wrapped around you

Butterfly Energy

It is time to spread your beautiful
wings & embrace the true you

Shadow Work

Work on your shadow self & come to terms
with your dark side as much as your light
side. In the darkness we can see our true light

The Sun Energy

Focus on the daily sun and ask that the sun helps you by sending you healing, codes and frequencies

Archangel's Healing Energy

A Beautiful gift from the Archangels
sending love, light and peace. Wrapping
all their wings around you now.

Archangel Sandalphon

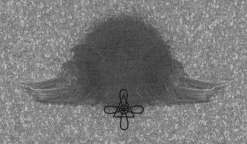

Archangel Sandalphon offers you comfort & grounding, with his wings wrapped around you.

Archangel Chamuel

Sending you unconditional love and compassion to your heart and helping your heart to feel lighter.

Heaven Above

Your loved ones in spirit are
around you and they send you lots
of love and comfort

The purple Ray of Light

Accept, receive and feel the clearing, cleansing and healing of your third eye

Mother Mary

大光明

Mother Mary is guiding you right now, she is by your side, share your worries with her and she will help you

Yeshua

'My child, I am here walking beside you. Release those tears and give them to me. I wrap you up in my pure white wings to comfort you'

Archangel Michael

I can be your strength and guide you in the right direction, just call on me and I will be there to help you.

Nature Realm

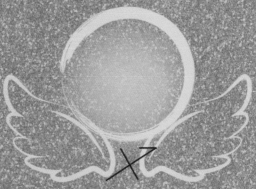

Spend more time in the natural world
and appreciate what nature has to offer
you

Mary Magdalene

Embrace your feminine side and learn to love who you are and be kind to yourself

Goddess Isis

'Shine bright my child and show the world the
true you'

Mother Earth

Be more In tune with the beauty of Mother
Earth & nature

Unicorn Energy

Learn to play again and create dreams that can become your reality

The Moon Energy

Be more in sync with the phases of
the moon. Use the moon energy to
bring you prosperity and good health

Archangel Michael

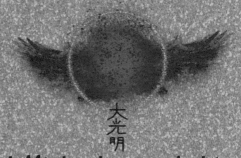

大光明

Archangel Michael spreads his beautiful wings around you and is comforting you at this time

Green Tara

Green Tara embraces you and is freeing
you from your constraints at this time

Archangel Uriel

You no longer need to carry the burdens of
the past, let them go and I will be there to
help you release and let them go

Archangel Gabriel

Call on me and share your concerns and
I will come forward to help you

Fairy Energy

Use our playful energy to help you to learn to
relax whether through music, dancing,
creative work or anything that makes you
laugh

The Cherubim's

Bringing fourth your wishes, make sure the cherubims hear exactly what you want

Archangel Uriel

Archangel Uriel sends you pure white
love energy and surrounds you in a
golden blue bubble

The Green Ray of Light

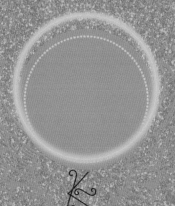

Embrace the green ray of light
filling your heart with
unconditional love

Heart Healing

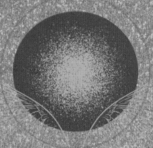

Meditate on the energy of the picture and
feel your heart being healed

Archangel Metatron

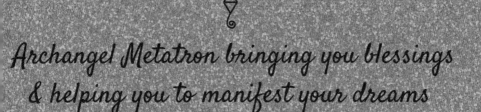

Archangel Metatron bringing you blessings
& helping you to manifest your dreams

Rebirth

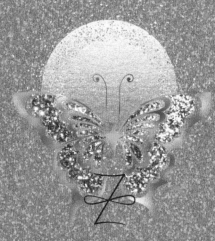

You are ready, believe in yourself & manifest your hopes and dreams

Dream State

Become more aware of your dreams
as they will help you in the awakened
life

The Pink Ray of Light

Embrace the pink ray of light within your body and surround yourself with unconditional love

Loved ones in Heaven

大光明

Your loved ones watch over you & they send you messages through the natural world feathers, birds, music and other sources. Be open to receive.

Archangel Sandalphon

Supporting your base chakra & helping you to stay grounded and focused

Night Sky

Spend time with the night-time stars
they bring comfort and healing joy for
you

The Sky Energy

Focus your attention on the sky and appreciate the beauty of the little things around you

Blue Ray of Light

Feel the throat chakra being cleared,
cleansed and renewed so you can speak
your truth

God Source Energy

Sending you Golden Lights of healing

Archangel Raphael

A gift from Archangel Raphael as she
wraps her green wings around you and
helping you at this time to heal old
wounds you no longer need.

The White Ray of Light

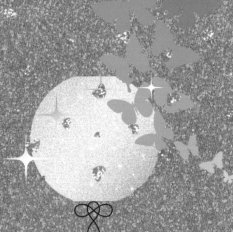

Allow the White ray of light to clear, cleanse and release anything that no longer serves you spritiually, mentally and emotionallly

Christ Light Energy

Embrace the enery of the Christ Light & feel it filling up your body

Mother Mary

I am filling you up with the blue energy of nurture to heal your inner child

44 oracle cards designed and channelled by me, these cards will help support & guide you. These cards have high frequency energy and codes to assist with healing the emotional, physical and mental body. They can be used as coasters, meditation or daily, guidance. They hold the most beautiful energy and I hope you will agree that these cards are magical ♥

Miss Kirsty E Pritchard
Nature Intuitive Energy Healer

Printed in Great Britain
by Amazon